Small but fierce unicorns. Noble and kind unicorns. Magical and untamable one-horned creatures . . .

Behold... the Unicorns!

Gail Gibbons

HarperCollinsPublishers

To Nancy Bryant and all
my friends at The Reading Corner Bookstore,
Rockland, Maine

Behold . . . the Unicorns!
Copyright © 2002 by Gail Gibbons
Printed in the U.S.A. All rights reserved.
www.harperchildrens.com
Library of Congress Cataloging-in-Publication Data
Gibbons, Gail.
Behold . . . the unicorns! / Gail Gibbons.
p.   cm.
ISBN 0-688-17955-X — ISBN 0-688-17958-4 (lib. bdg.)
1. Unicorns—Juvenile literature. [1. Unicorns.]
GR830.U6 G5   2002   398.24´54—dc21   00-049880   CIP   AC
Typography by Stephanie Bart-Horvath
1 2 3 4 5 6 7 8 9 10
❖
First Edition

Around the world people have told stories about the fabulous creatures called unicorns. These stories, retold and passed down through time, are called legends. Legends may have a basis in fact, or they may be imaginary—or both!

The word *unicorn* comes from the Latin word *unicornis,* which means "one horn." All unicorns, real or imaginary, have something in common—they each have one horn.

RHINOCEROS

SKELETON OF
MONOCLONIUS

About 120 million years ago there lived
a dinosaur unicorn. It didn't look
anything like the unicorns we imagine,
but it did have one horn on its head.

The narwhal is sometimes called a sea unicorn. Actually its horn is a tooth that has grown into a long, spiraled tusk. The Indian rhinoceros is a present-day unicorn. Perhaps long ago these creatures inspired stories of imaginary unicorns.

NARWHAL

INDIAN RHINOCEROS

People in many cultures believed the strength of an animal was centered in the horns it used for protection. When the animal had only one horn, the horn was seen as twice as powerful—and magical!

Unicorns of legend vary in size, shape, and color.

PERSIA

THIS CHINESE UNICORN HAS A SHORT, CURLY HORN.

GREECE

ENGLAND

One unicorn wasn't an animal at all. In India long ago, stories were told about Risharinga, the son of a Hindu priest. Risharinga was a handsome and innocent young man who lived deep in the woods. From his forehead grew a single horn.

Back then a greedy king so angered the gods that they punished him by making sure no rain would fall. Soon there was a terrible drought and people were dying. It was the goodness of Risharinga that saved them all. He wept with sorrow when he saw such suffering, and immediately a hard rain poured from the heavens.

In ancient China unicorns were often magical gift givers. This story was told of the wise emperor Fu Hsi. A unicorn, the *ki-lin,* rose from a river and offered the emperor a package it was carrying on its back. It was said that the gift from the *ki-lin* contained symbols that taught the Chinese people their first written words.

For centuries the people of Arabia and Persia told stories about the Karkaddan. This creature was said to have had the magical ability to take on different forms. Sometimes the Karkaddan was portrayed as mean and violent, but in other stories he was better tempered. It was said of the Karkaddan that when it dipped its horn in poisoned water, the water became pure.

About 2500 years ago a Greek named Ctesias (TEE-see-us) was living in Persia. He listened as merchants and travelers told stories of their adventures in Asia. They spoke of a wondrous one-horned creature that lived in India.

Ctesias wrote the stories down. He described the unicorn's colorful horn, which was said to possess magical powers capable of ridding the body of poisons and of curing dreaded diseases. This was the first written description of a unicorn.

THE *RE-EM* MAY HAVE BEEN AN AFRICAN ANTELOPE CALLED THE ORYX, OR *RIM* IN ARABIC. IT HAS TWO HORNS!

About two hundred years later a group of scholars was translating the Hebrew Bible into Greek. They found seven mentions of a mysterious and powerful animal called the *re-em*. What could this be? Finally they decided that the *re-em* was actually a unicorn. The writers of the Hebrew Bible did not believe in unicorns, but the mistake in translation was made.

From then on, unicorns became part of all sorts of religious stories. These stories were collected into manuscripts and illustrated with beautiful art. Preachers would use them to teach people about Christianity.

One such story was about Adam and Eve in the Garden of Eden. When God told Adam to name all the creatures of the earth, Adam picked the unicorn to name first. As thunder shook the heavens, God reached down and touched the unicorn's horn. That was a sign it was blessed above all creatures.

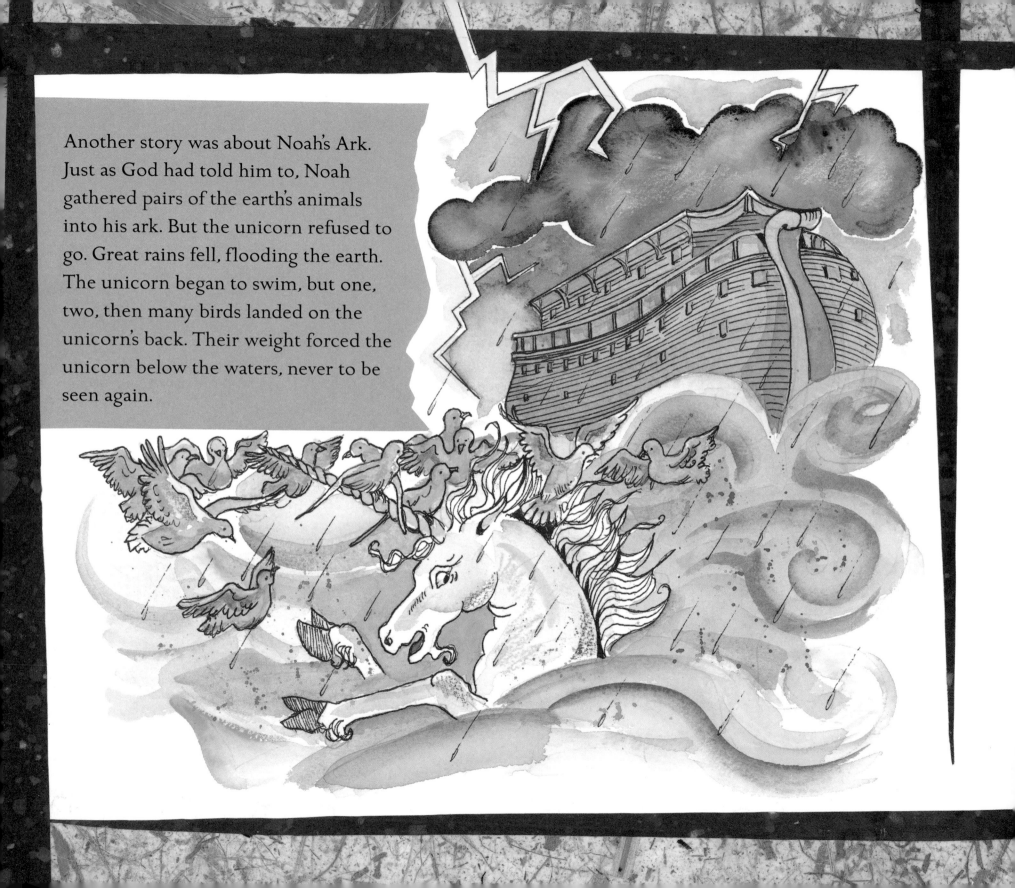

Another story was about Noah's Ark. Just as God had told him to, Noah gathered pairs of the earth's animals into his ark. But the unicorn refused to go. Great rains fell, flooding the earth. The unicorn began to swim, but one, two, then many birds landed on the unicorn's back. Their weight forced the unicorn below the waters, never to be seen again.

SIRENAE

GRIFFIN

UNICORNIS

In the Middle Ages people could also read about unicorns in bestiaries. These were collections of information about real and imaginary animals. People readily believed that unicorns were real.

One bestiary said that unicorns could be lured by an innocent young maiden. In an old Russian legend a dreaded disease called typhoid struck down a village. Katya, a fair maiden, sat quietly, softly singing, hoping to attract a unicorn. One indeed did appear, and placed its head on her lap.

The unicorn purified the water in the village and held its horn over those who were ill until they were cured. All was well until the greedy villagers killed the creature for its magical horn. When typhoid came again, the unicorn's horn failed to save them.

In Europe one medieval king, Charles VI of France, was obsessed with capturing a unicorn. Stories told of wild people who lived in a vast dark wood. Best of all, they rode on the backs of unicorns! King Charles made many attempts to trick the wild people and their unicorns out of hiding, but he always failed.

THE HUNT BEGINS

PURIFYING THE STREAM

LEAPING THE STREAM

About that time great tapestries were woven to adorn the walls of castles and rich people's homes. The most famous is a series of seven tapestries called *The Hunt of the Unicorn*. The images in the tapestries are filled with Christian beliefs and symbols.

The seven tapestries tell the story of a unicorn being hunted, tamed by a maiden, and then killed. The people of medieval Europe would have understood that these images were also telling another kind of story.

TAMING OF THE UNICORN

THE UNICORN FIGHTS

THE UNICORN IS KILLED

THE UNICORN LIVES

The unicorn surely represents goodness and strength. In the last panel we can see that it is alive again, living in a beautiful garden. Some say the unicorn represents the promise of heaven. But we will never know for sure.

In the Middle Ages European merchants sold unicorn horns—or so they said. Kings, queens, and wealthy people treasured the horns, believing they held the magical power of unicorns. Fearing poison, they would have a servant touch each goblet and dish with the horn to purify the contents. They didn't know that the horns were really the tusks of narwhals!

Brave kings and medieval knights sought to fight against their enemies with the speed and courage of unicorns. They too believed that unicorns symbolized goodness and strength. Images of unicorns adorned shields, flags, banners, and appeared on castle carvings too.

Today the images of unicorns appear everywhere. Unicorns go up and down on merry-go-rounds. They decorate music boxes, jewelry, greeting cards, and clothing. We also see them in children's books and movies.

The unicorn still represents the qualities most people value. They are seen as being gentle, brave, strong, kind, and noble creatures. They live around the edges of our imagination and in our legends. Behold . . . the unicorns!

UNICORN FOOTPRINTS

For centuries Scotland and England were at war. In this well-known nursery rhyme the lion symbolizes England and the unicorn symbolizes Scotland.

The lion and the unicorn
Were fighting for the crown.
The lion chased the unicorn
All around the town.

About five hundred years ago doctors sold powdered "unicorn" horn as medicine to cure all ills.

The horn of the Indian rhinoceros isn't made of bone. It's made of keratin, a protein found in fingernails. This rhinoceros is endangered, which means there aren't many left.

Today *The Hunt of the Unicorn* can be seen at the Cloisters Museum in New York City. The museum is dedicated to the art of medieval times.

Stories of one-horned creatures may have come from Egyptian wall carvings that show people and creatures from the side—like this oryx that really is a two-horned animal.